Fantastic Mr Fox

by Roald Dahl

Adapted for the stage by
David Wood

Samuel French — London
New York - Toronto - Hollywood

ISBN 0 573 05133 X

Please see page viii for further copyright information

FANTASTIC MR FOX

Commissioned by the Belgrade Theatre, Coventry, and first performed there on 3rd April, 2001, with the following cast:

Badger/Narrator	Barry Woolgar
Mr Fox	Alex Lowe
Mrs Fox/Mabel	Carmelle McAree
Boggis	Nick Walker
Bunce	Paul Nolan
Bean/Rat	Mike Kirchner
Mrs Badger	Katy Stephens

Community Cast:

Young Farmer/Mr Mole	Daniel Metcalfe
Young Farmer/Mr Weasel	Aaron Harris
Young Farmer/Mr Rabbit	Shane Robson
Young Farmer/Rat	Marcus Morrison
Young Farmer/Rat	Ricardo Morgan
Young Farmer	Reece Platt-May
Mrs Mole	Sarah Burdekin
Small Moles	Kerri Byrne
	Craig Nolan
	Lee Anthony Scott
	Teri Upton
Mrs Weasel	Hannah Bains
Small Weasels	Nikita Jaspal
	Lahna Patel
	Rebekah Darke
	Sarah Darke
Mrs Rabbit	Leanne Meaney
Small Rabbits	Lucy Ashby
	Kyle Ashford

	Grace Healey
	Natasha Jackson
Small Badgers	David Crews
	Rachel Lowe
	Martin Wallis
	David Kenny
	Kayleigh Power
Small Foxes	Keith Hands
	Arthur Haynes
	George Hanes
	Lucy Wooton
Landgirls	Rebecca Brinkley
	Kira Danielle Ashford
	Kate Halpin
	Jennifer Lees
	Kate Stoney
	Nicola Simms
Landgirl/Rat	Angharad Gibbs
Chaperones	Margaret Blumson
	Diane Majrowski
	Anna Norris
	Lisa McDonald
Villagers	Barbara Pickering
	Jean Gill
	Coral Romer
	Diane Arnold
	Netta McIlroy
	Joan Rennie

Producer **Jane Hytch**
Director **Kathi Leahy**
Designer **Keith Baker**
Composer **John Kirkpatrick**
Choreographer **Jill Freeman**
Lighting Designer **Bennie Howe**
Sound Designer **Steve Wilson**

CHARACTERS

Badger/Narrator, avuncularly friendly
Mr Fox, confidently courageous
Mrs Fox, bravely protective
Boggis, a fat farmer
Bunce, a "pot-bellied dwarf" farmer
Bean, a lean, tall farmer
Rat, whinging parasite
Mabel, gossipy housekeeper
Four Small Foxes and **One Small Badger**, speaking
roles for children

One of the Farmers can double Rat; Mrs Fox can double
Mabel.

Supernumerary Animals
Mrs Badger
Two More Small Badgers
Mole
Mrs Mole
Four Small Moles
Rabbit
Mrs Rabbit
Five Small Rabbits
Weasel
Mrs Weasel
Six Small Weasels
Three Rats (in **Bean**'s cellar only)

N.B. The **Animals** can, if necessary, also play **Villagers**
in one scene.

All the Supernumerary Animals form the "Animal Audience" who are guests at the feast. They react to the story and play parts as required.

Supernumerary Human Beings
Farm Workers (say 10)
Villagers (say 10)—could be played by the **Animals**

Perhaps a Musician, possibly playing one of the Supernumerary Animals, could play a squeezebox or a violin—a country/folk sound, to be augmented with percussion instruments played by other Supernumerary Animals.

SYNOPSIS OF SCENES

ACT I

TABLETOP	For celebratory dance, plus setting up of characters and start of story
FOXHOLE	Night
TABLETOP	Under tree, night
FOXHOLE	Night
TABLETOP	Under tree, day
FOXHOLE	Digging
TABLETOP	Under tree, day—Optional
UNDERGROUND	Night
TABLETOP	Under tree/UNDERGROUND—major scene leading to tree falling, night

ACT II

TABLETOP	Celebration—story resumption— Farmers' camp, day
UNDERGROUND	
TABLETOP	Boggis's shed
UNDERGROUND/TABLETOP	For starving animals— Badger's lament
UNDERGROUND	
TABLETOP	Bunce's store
UNDERGROUND	
TABLETOP	Bean's cellar
UNDERGROUND	
TABLETOP	Feast/Farmers' finale/final celebration

ACKNOWLEDGEMENTS

David Wood wishes to thank Bob Eaton and Jane Hytch
of The Belgrade Theatre, Coventry, for commissioning
this play and Kathi Leahy for directing such a splendid
production.

Music
The original music commissioned by The Belgrade
Theatre from John Kirkpatrick is not currently available
but please address any enquiries to The Editorial
Department at Samuel French Ltd.

Cover Illustration
The cover illustration is by Quentin Blake and remains his
copyright. Any enquiries regarding its use should be
addressed to his agent A.P. Watt Ltd, 20 John Street,
London, WC1N 2DR.

Samuel French Ltd acknowledges the publication of the
original book *Fantastic Mr Fox* by Roald Dahl, published
in the UK by Puffin Books.

INTRODUCTION

When I read *Fantastic Mr Fox* with a view to adapting it from page to stage, my favourite image, enhanced by Quentin Blake's illustration, was the celebration hosted by the Fox family. Sitting round a feast-laden table are the Badger, Mole, Rabbit and Weasel families—parents and children.

To recreate that magical scene required a core of half a dozen experienced actors and a chorus of celebrating animals of all ages who have no individual lines.

Jane Hytch and Kathi Leahy, who commissioned the adaptation for the Belgrade Theatre, Coventry, were able to provide the ideal production structure. I could use six professional actors joined by a community cast of as many as fifty or sixty adults and children.

The main roles could all be played (with some doubling) by the professionals. And I could have not only enough community cast to play the chorus of animals, but also a team of Farmworkers and Villagers.

The story celebrates rural life and the triumph of the animals over the control-freak human beings. So I wrote the play as a festive celebration (as described at the end of the book) in which all the "digging" animals toast Mr Fox. As part of the celebration, Badger narrates the story of how Mr Fox outwitted the Farmers and the other animals at the party participate and help create the story.

However, the animals do not play the three human (inhuman) Farmers. They are "conjured up" by the Narrator in their real human hideousness.

I envisaged music played live by one or more of the supernumerary animals—folk-style music played on a squeezebox or violin plus percussion. The original production used delightfully appropriate music specially written by John Kirkpatrick; it was pre-recorded, which worked fine.

The Belgrade decided to employ another professional actor to play Mrs Badger. She became a co-narrator. This was acceptable, and the performance was excellent; but I would have preferred to retain the clear focus provided by one narrator, and so have not incorporated her enhanced role in this script.

My favourite image from the book—the feast—led me to imagine the action of the play taking place on a huge, raked tabletop, on which or around which the animal audience sit and watch. Such a platform would be impractical for some productions. Maybe the stage itself could be made to represent the tabletop.

Ideally two levels are needed, to suggest overground and underground. The tabletop could be used for the overground acting area, as well as for the interiors of the Farmers' stores and sheds. These could be created with flown-in flats or by members of the "animal audience" standing and holding prop chickens, geese, cider jars, etc., or they could hold up painted backcloths.

The underground area would ideally be under the tabletop, perhaps revealed by a revolve. Alternatively it could be on auditorium level, "below" the stage, if visibility is reasonable. Another possibility is a curtained area below the raised platform. Ideally trapdoors would link overground and underground.

Alternatively, it would be possible to imaginatively use one space for both overground and underground. Lighting could help identify each area. A cyc. surrounding the stage could offer sky effects for night and day overground, and interesting shapes and shadows for underground. Other exciting lightning possibilities include a possible strobe effect for the slow motion falling of the tree, and a lightning/rain effect towards the end.

The tree (which has to appear and also fall to the ground) could be flown in or slotted into the tabletop; this may be impractical if the tabletop is to revolve. Maybe it is *behind* the tabletop.

When the Farmhands surround the foxhole, they could be in the auditorium.

Access to the tabletop is necessary from the upstage wings, for the entrances of the Farmers and their tractors/shovels.

When the animals are at the feast, the food could be painted on or attached to a tablecloth, which could be removed when the animals dance and the story is played out on the tabletop.

The original production design inventively used a revolving structure giving levels; the stage was not the tabletop, but the feast took place in front of the structure. A network of tunnels and trapdoors was skilfully created, using all the Belgrade's resources. I'm sure that companies with less sophisticated facilities will find equally effective ways of presenting the play.

David Wood

OTHER PLAYS AND MUSICALS BY DAVID WOOD

Aladdin
The BFG (based on the book by Roald Dahl)
Babe, the Sheep-Pig (based on the book by Dick King-Smith)
Babes in the Magic Wood
Cinderella
Dick Whittington and Wondercat
Dinosaurs and all that Rubbish (based on the book by Michael Foreman)
Flibberty and the Penguin
The Gingerbread Man
Hijack Over Hygenia
The Ideal Gnome Expedition
Jack and the Giant
Jack the Lad (co-written with Dave and Toni Arthur)
Larry the Lamb in Toytown (co-written with Sheila Ruskin, adapted from
the stories of S. G. Hulme-Beaman)
Meg and Mog Show (from the books by Helen Nicoll and Jan Pienkowski)
More Adventures of Noddy (based on the stories by Enid Blyton)
Mother Goose's Golden Christmas
Noddy (based on the stories by Enid Blyton)
Nutcracker Sweet
Old Father Time
The Old Man of Lochnagar (based on the book by HRH The Prince of Wales)
Old Mother Hubbard
The Owl and the Pussycat went to See... (co-written with Sheila Ruskin)
The Papertown Paperchase
The Pied Piper (co-written with Dave and Toni Arthur)
The Plotters of Cabbage Patch Corner
Robin Hood (co-written with Dave and Toni Arthur)
Rupert and the Green Dragon (based on the Rupert stories and characters
by Mary Tourtel and Alfred Bestall)
Save the Human (based on the story by Tony Husband and David Wood)
The See-Saw Tree
The Selfish Shellfish
Spot's Birthday Party (based on the books by Eric Hill)
There Was An Old Woman...
Tickle (one act)
Tom's Midnight Garden (based on the book by Philippa Pearce)
The Twits (based on the book by Roald Dahl)
The Witches (based on the book by Roald Dahl)

Theatre for Children—Guide to Writing, Adapting, Directing and Acting
(written with Janet Grant, published by Faber and Faber)

ACT I

As the audience arrive, the tabletop is in view. Round the edge are drinking vessels. In the centre lie the remains of a feast on a tablecloth

Music strikes up—homespun folk music. With the House Lights up, the entire company of animals dances through the auditorium, whooping excitedly and encouraging the audience to clap in rhythm

As the animals reach the stage, they remove the tablecloth and clamber on to the tabletop to dance joyfully

The House Lights fade

The adult and teenage animals dance an exuberant country dance while the younger animals play, chasing each other through the dancers

All cheer as the dance comes to an end. Badger steps forward and gestures for quiet

Badger My friends! My fellow diggers!
All (*like a football chant, with gestures*) Digga digga dig!
              Digga digga dig!
              Digga digga digga digga
              Dig dig dig!
Badger The burrowing Rabbits!

The Rabbit family assembles in a group

Rabbits Digga digga dig!
Badger The mining Moles!

The Mole family assembles

Moles Digga digga dig!
Badger The scrabbling Weasels!

The Weasel family assembles

Weasels Digga digga dig!
Badger The excavating Badgers!

Badger's family gathers round him

Badgers Digga digga dig!
Badger And last but most definitely not least, the tunnelling Foxes!

The Fox family assembles

Foxes Digga digga dig!
Badger You are all most welcome!
All   Digga digga dig!
              Digga digga dig!
              Digga digga digga digga
              Dig dig dig!
Badger Have you had a good feast?
All (*enthusiastically*) Aaaaaah!

Weasel burps loudly. Laughter as his wife scolds him

Badger Pray be seated!

All except Badger take their seats around the tabletop

It's time to say a big thank you...
Young Animals (*shouting*) THANK YOU!
Badger (*laughing*) Not yet, not yet! A big thank you to the greatest digger
of us all, without whom we wouldn't be here today. My dear friend, Foxy!

All cheer. Fox stands and acknowledges the ovation

Some of you may know his story. Some of you may not. But please, listen,
(*taking in the audience*) everybody, while I tell it. This is the tale of...
FANTASTIC MR FOX!
All FANTASTIC MR FOX!

*The adult animals drink a toast as music introduces the story. From now on
the animals climb up on to the tabletop to act out the story as required.
Incidental music and sound effects can be provided by the seated animal
audience*

Badger On a hill above the valley there was a wood. In the wood there was
a huge tree.

Music, as the tree is revealed or positioned US *of the tabletop*

Under the tree there was a hole. In the hole lived Mr Fox and Mrs Fox and their four Small Foxes.

The Fox family assemble beneath the tree

Every evening, as soon as it got dark, Mr Fox would say:

Mr Fox Well, my darlings, what shall it be for supper tonight? A plump chicken? A juicy goose? A succulent duck? Or a tasty turkey?

The Fox family huddle together, miming their discussion

Badger Once they had decided, Mr Fox would creep through the darkness down into the valley…

Music as Mr Fox waves goodbye to his family, who return to their seats or go behind the tree. Mr Fox stealthily creeps around the tabletop, then lurks in the shadows

In the valley were three farms. They belonged to three of the richest, nastiest, most loathsome farmers you could ever wish not to meet…

The three farmers enter from US *and assemble on the tabletop. Boggis carries a chicken, Bunce carries a duck and a goose, Bean carries a turkey and a flagon of cider*

As they approach, self-satisfied and smarmy, the animal audience start hissing their disapproval. When chickens, ducks, geese and turkeys are mentioned in the following rhymes, the animal children make appropriate noises

Bunce   I'm Bunce,
Bean   I'm Bean,
Boggis   I'm Boggis,
             My chickens are best (*holding up the chicken*), look at that!
             For lunch and for tea
             I always eat three
             With dumplings…
Several Animal Children …no wonder you're fat!

The animals laugh. Boggis reacts angrily

Bean   I'm Bean,

Boggis   I'm Boggis,
Bunce   I'm Bunce,
              My ducks and my geese are so big!
              I love stuffing my face
              With goose-liver paste
              And I...
Several Animal Children ...look like a pot-bellied pig!

The animals laugh. Bunce reacts angrily

Boggis   I'm Boggis,
Bunce   I'm Bunce,
Bean   I'm Bean,
              My turkeys are choice, they're the pick!
              And I make cider you know
              From the apples I grow
              And...
Several Animal Children ...you're always as tight as a tick!

The animals laugh. Bean reacts angrily

Farmers We are the greatest!

The animals boo. The farmers drop their chicken, goose, duck, turkey and cider to the ground and advance menacingly on the animal audience. They are stopped in their tracks by the animal children chanting

Animal Children Boggis and Bunce and Bean
              One fat, one short, one lean.
              These horrible crooks
              So different in looks
              Were nonetheless equally mean!

The adult animals join in as the farmers shake their fists furiously. During the chanting, Mr Fox creeps round behind the farmers and steals the chicken, goose, duck, turkey and cider, popping it all into a sack

Animals   Boggis and Bunce and Bean
              One fat, one short, one lean.
              These horrible crooks
              So different in looks
              Were nonetheless equally mean!
Boggis Shut up you leaky chot...

The others look at him

...you cheeky lot.
Bunce Vermin!
Bean Parasites!
Boggis Ge'll wet you!

The others look at him

(*Angrily*) We'll get you! Nobody laughs at us!

Behind the farmers, Mr Fox cheekily mimes laughing at them. The animal audience join in

Bunce Nobody makes us look silly!
Bean We are farmers. We are cool!
Boggis Yes! We are farmers. We are fools!
Bunce & Bean No!

They pull Boggis away and all turn US. *Mr Fox retreats into the shadows. The farmers go to pick up their things, but find them gone*

Farmers (*spluttering with rage*) B-b-b-b-but wh-wh-wh-wh-where c-c-c-c-can... Aaaaagh!

The animals laugh as the farmers throw themselves into a huddle and freeze DS

Music as Mr Fox emerges from the shadows and returns to the tree, under which Mrs Fox and the Fox children meet him

Badger Then clever Mr Fox would return to his wife and children, show them the rewards of his cunning and prepare to share a scrumptious supper.

Mr Fox shows his family the contents of his sack and they all excitedly descend into their foxhole (down a trap door in the tabletop), as the Lighting on them fades

Night after night after night, Boggis, Bunce and Bean were fooled by Mr Fox.

The farmers unfreeze. The Light on them brightens

Dang and blast that lousy, thieving beast!

Bunce I'd like to rip his guts out!

Bean He must be killed!

Boggis But how? How on earth can we catch the blighter!

Bean (*picking his nose thoughtfully*) I have a plan.

Bunce You've never had a decent plan yet.

Bean Shut up and listen. Tomorrow night we will all hide just outside the hole where the fox lives. We will wait there until he comes out. Then... (*Miming a shotgun*) Bang! Bang-bang-bang!

Boggis Very clever.

Bunce But first we shall have to find the hole.

Bean My dear Bunce, I've already found it.

Sinister music

It's up in the wood on the hill. It's under a huge tree.

The farmers cackle evilly and start to exit. The animals start to boo

The farmers cackle more, shake their fists and exit

The Lighting fades

As Badger narrates, the foxhole is revealed (the tabletop revolves or a curtain is drawn back)

Badger The next night, cosy in their foxhole, unaware of the farmers' evil plan, the Fox family relaxed.

The Fox children are playing a game. (Snap, perhaps? Or twister? Or a game of rough and tumble with their father.)

Mr Fox Well, my darling, what shall it be tonight?

The fox children play noisily or laugh

Mrs Fox Hush, children. I can't hear myself think. (*She thinks*) Ah yes! I think we'll have duck tonight. Bring us two fat ducks, if you please. One for you and me, and one for the children.

Mr Fox Duck it shall be! Bunce's best. (*He prepares to leave*)

Mrs Fox Now do be careful.

Mr Fox My darling, I can smell those foul farmers a mile away. I can even smell one from the other.

The children become interested

Boggis gives off a filthy stink of rotten chicken skins.
Fox Children Pooooh!
Mr Fox Bunce reeks of goose livers.
Fox Children Uggggh!
Mr Fox And as for Bean, the fumes of apple cider hang around him like poisonous gases!
Fox Children Yuck!
Mrs Fox Yes, but just don't get careless.
Mr Fox Don't you worry about me! I'll see you later.
Fox Children Bye, Dad!
Mr & Mrs Fox Bye!

Mr Fox starts to go as the Lights fade

The scene changes back to under the tree. Moonlight

The three farmers enter stealthily to sinister music. They enter in a line, shotguns raised

When the front one stops, the guns poke in the front and middle farmers' backs. They jump and drop their shotguns

All Shhhh!

They pick up their shotguns. Bean indicates to the others to surround the hole. They face inwards. Boggis points his gun towards Bean

Bean (*whispering*) Boggis, put it down!
Boggis What?
Bean The gun. Down!

Boggis drops it on his foot

Boggis Ow!
Bunce & Bean Shhhh!
Bean No! *Point* it down. Don't point it at me! Point it at the hole!
Boggis What hole?
Bunce & Bean The foxhole!

All stand poised, aiming their shotguns

Bunce Now. Stand by!

Tension music as the trap door slowly opens and Mr Fox starts to emerge

Perhaps the animal children start to whisper a warning. Perhaps the audience pick this up and start shouting. Mr Fox is nearly out of the trapdoor. Suddenly Bean turns on a torch and lights up Mr Fox's face. He freezes

Bean Fire!

Mr Fox makes for the trapdoor as the shotguns fire. The farmers rush to the hole

Mr Fox exits, leaving his tail

Bunce Did we get him?
Boggis We got him! We got him!

Bean shines the torch and picks up Mr Fox's tail. Mr Fox has gone

Bean This is the tail of the fox ... ha! But where's the rest of him?
Boggis Dang and blast! We shot too late! We should have let fly the moment he poked his head out!
Bunce Never mind. Shows him we mean business.
Bean Unfinished business!
Boggis Are you listening, Mr Fox? This is only the beginning!

Laughing maniacally, the farmers turn, bump into each other, and exit arguing to the boos of the animals and, hopefully, the audience

The scene changes back to inside the foxhole. Mr Fox's family surround him as Mrs Fox tends his stump

Mrs Fox It was the finest tail for miles around.
Mr Fox Oof! It hurts.
Mrs Fox It's bound to, my love. But it'll soon get better.
Fox Child 1 And it'll soon grow again, Dad.
Fox Child 2 Yes, you'll get another one.
Mr Fox (*shaking his head*) No, children. It will never grow again. I shall be tailless for the rest of my life.
Fox Child 3 Cheer up, Dad.
Fox Child 4 At least you're home!
Mr Fox (*smiling*) Indeed I am. Oh, if only I hadn't been so stupid. I was sure it was safe. Not the slightest whiff of a farmer. Then, bang bang, the entire wood seemed to explode around me. Stupid.
Mrs Fox (*finishing tending the stump*) There. Now, children, there's no food tonight, so it's early to bed.
Fox Children Oh, Mum!

Mrs Fox Try to sleep.

The children settle, as do their parents

Mr Fox Sorry children. I'll be back on form tomorrow. Night.
Fox Children Night, Dad. Night, Mum.

*Music as they fall asleep. Mr and Mrs Fox look encouragingly at each other,
as the Lights fade*

    On the tabletop, Badger appears

Badger The three farmers decided not to wait for Mr Fox to venture from
his foxhole again. But they didn't give up their vengeful campaign. Far
from it. They came back ... with their shovels.

*The farmers enter, shovels over their shoulders silhouetted against the
moonlit sky*

The animals start to chant

Animals (*starting softly, rising to a climax*) Boggis and Bunce and Bean
           One fat, one short, one lean.
           These horrible crooks
           So different in looks
           Were nonetheless equally mean!
Farmers (*wielding their shovels*) Poxy fox we know you're there,
           We'll dig you out, we will we swear!

*Music as they start to mime digging. The shovels strike the tabletop
threateningly*

*Lights up in the foxhole. The farmers are still digging above. The Fox family
is asleep, but suddenly Mr Fox wakes with a start. He listens to the sound
coming from above*

Mr Fox (*suddenly realizing*) Wake up! Wake up!

The family awakes with a start

Mrs Fox What is it? What is it?
Mr Fox Shhh. (*He listens*)

They all listen

They're digging us out!
Mrs Fox (*terrified*) What? Are you sure?
Mr Fox Positive. Listen.
Mrs Fox They'll kill my children!
Mr Fox Never.
Mrs Fox They will. They will.

The fox children huddle up to their parents

Fox Children Mum! Dad!
Mr Fox It's all right, children. Stay calm.
Mrs Fox Calm? How can we stay calm?
Fox Child 1 How will they kill us, Mum?
Fox Child 2 Will there be dogs?

Mrs Fox begins to sob and clasps her children to her. Mr Fox decisively moves nearer the noise. Suddenly a shovel breaks through from above, nearly hitting him. The farmers cheer. Mr Fox dashes back to the others

Mr Fox We've got to dig! All of us! Come on! We can dig faster than any farmer! Nobody in the world can dig as quick as a fox!

Galvanised into action and led by Mr Fox, the fox family start digging. This is an energetic, stylised mime, accompanied by a musical pulse (part of which is still the menacing noise of the shovels), and the chanting of the animals round the tabletop giving their support

Animals   Digga digga dig!
               Digga digga dig!
               Digga digga digga digga
               Dig dig dig!

               Digga digga dig!
               Digga digga dig!
               Digga digga digga digga
               Dig dig dig!

Mr Fox (*yelling encouragement*) Dig down! Dig deep!
               Deep as we possibly can!

Animals   Digga digga dig!
               Digga digga dig!
               Digga digga digga digga
               Dig dig dig!

Digga digga dig!
Digga digga dig!
Digga digga digga digga
Dig dig dig!

The farmers digging above have slowed down, showing signs of tiredness, but they carry on their mime, almost in slow motion. Their shovels no longer make any noise

Mr Fox Hold it!

The Fox family stop digging. They rest, panting with breathless determination

Badger is seen on the tabletop

Badger After about an hour the Fox Family looked back up the long tunnel they had dug.
Mr Fox Shh! Shh!

All listen. Then...

Phew! I think we've done it! They'll never get as deep as this.
Mrs Fox You mean we're safe?
Mr Fox Safe! Well done, everyone! Well dug!

The Fox children (and the animals) cheer with relief. They all sit down to rest. Mr Fox smiles. Mrs Fox hugs him. The Lighting fades on the foxhole and brightens on the tabletop

The farmers are still digging, but slowly and with great effort

Badger As the sun rose next morning, Boggis and Bunce and Bean were still digging. They had dug a hole so deep you could have put a house into it. But they hadn't reached the end of the foxes' tunnel.
Boggis Dang and blast! *(Threateningly to Bunce)* Whose rotten idea was this?
Bunce Bean's idea.
Boggis Bean! *(He turns to Bean)*

Boggis's shovel, over his shoulder, strikes Bunce on the back of the head

Bunce Ow! Clodhopper!

Boggis turns back to Bunce

Boggis Sorry…

Boggis's shovel hits Bean on the back of the head

Bean Ow! Pot-walloper!

Boggis turns back to Bean

Boggis Sorry…

This time Bunce ducks, so Boggis's shovel goes over his head. He raises his head just in time to be smacked in the face as Boggis swings his shovel back

Bunce Ow! Bog-trotter!
Bean Shut up and listen!

Boggis and Bunce turn to Bean

I want that fox! I'm going to get that fox! I'm not giving in till I've strung him up over my front porch, dead as a dumpling!
Boggis We can't get him by digging, that's for sure. I've had enough of digging.
Bunce (*to Bean*) Have you got any more stupid ideas then?

Bean starts to react violently, but thinks better of it. He beckons. The farmers gather in a plotting huddle

Badger As the farmers plotted their next move, the villagers came up the hill and looked at the vast hole.

Music as the animals leave their seats to play villagers. They look sadly down from the tabletop

Villagers (*with feeling*) Boggis and Bunce and Bean,
          Look what they've done, its obscene.
          They couldn't care less
          They've made all this mess
          Where everything used to be green.

A still pause

Suddenly the farmers break from their huddle

Farmers Got it!

Villager Hey there, Boggis. What's going on?
Boggis We're after a fox!
Villagers You must be mad!

The farmers advance on the villagers

Boggis Shove off, the lot of you!

The villagers scatter and return to their seats

Bunce Goody goody do-gooders!
Bean Death to the fox!
Farmers Death to the fox!

The animals boo as the farmers turn to go and bump into each other

Then Bunce and Bean exit, leaving Boggis looking down the hole

Badger While Boggis stayed on guard, Bunce and Bean prepared the next
stage of their cruel campaign. Meanwhile the Fox family felt safe enough
to rest.

Music as Lighting reveals the foxhole. Mr Fox is asleep

Fox Child 1 Mum, have the farmers gone?
Mrs Fox I think so.
Fox Child 2 Are we really safe?
Mrs Fox I think so. Now, hush. Your dad's asleep. If it wasn't for him we'd
all be dead by now. Your father is a fantastic fox.
Fox Children (*sleepily*) A fantastic fox.
Mrs Fox (*singing*) Deep in the ground
                         Though hungry and fearful
                         We're trying
                         To stay brave and cheerful,
                         Deep in the ground
                         Sleep sound
                         And dream of a better day tomorrow.

The animals hum a vocal backing

                         Deep in the ground
                         We've still got each other
                         Four sisters and brothers

Their father and mother,
Deep in the ground
Sleep sound
And dream of a better day tomorrow.

Music continues as the foxes settle to sleep. The animals reprise the song

After a couple of lines, as a sinister counterpoint to the comforting lullaby, a team of farm workers enters from US

It is dark, so at first all we see is the light of the torches they carry. Their leader hands Boggis his shotgun. Boggis then directs the farm workers to stand around the foxhole. This involves them going into the auditorium and positioning themselves all around

Animals (*singing*) Deep in the ground
Though hungry and fearful
They're trying
To stay brave and cheerful,
Deep in the ground
Sleep sound
And dream of a better day tomorrow.

Deep in the ground
They've still got each other
Four sisters and brothers
Their father and mother,
Deep in the ground
Sleep sound
And dream of a better day tomorrow.

Deep in the ground
Though hungry and fearful
They're trying
To stay brave and cheerful,
Deep in the ground
Sleep sound
And dream of a better day tomorrow.

The song ends and the farm workers are ready in position. Tension music. Boggis steps forward

Boggis Hey there, Poxy Foxy. Can you hear me? You're surrounded!

You've had it! You've had your last chicken too. You'll never come prowling round my farm again. (*He calls*) Bunce! Bean! Do your worst! Death to the fox!

The sudden terrible roar of engines rents the air. From us *enter Bunce and Bean, driving tractors equipped with mechanical shovels with glinting metallic teeth*

They menacingly approach the edge of the tabletop, then start digging. Mechanical clanks and clangs. Boggis excitedly watches. After a while the Foxes below start to wake up

Fox Children Dad, Dad! Mum, Mum!
Fox Child 1 What's happening, Dad?
Fox Child 2 What are they doing?
Mrs Fox It's an earthquake!

Mrs Fox and the children scream. Mr Fox goes to look and listen

Mr Fox Tractors! And mechanical shovels! Dig for your lives! Dig, dig, dig! Diiiiiiiiiig!

The roar of the machinery continues, joined by the animals chanting. The fox family mime digging even more feverishly than before

Animals   Digga digga dig!
                  Digga digga dig!
                  Digga digga digga digga
                  Dig dig dig!

                  Digga digga dig!
                  Digga digga dig!
                  Digga digga digga digga
                  Dig dig dig!
Mr Fox Faster, faster!
Boggis Faster, faster!
Foxes Faster, faster!
Farmers & Farm Workers Faster, faster!
Foxes & Animals Faster, faster!

One fox child, the smallest, has become detached from the group. He remains c *as the others head for the* ds *exit*

Suddenly all the noise ceases except for a musical pulse for tension. The action changes to slow motion. The mechanical shovels, the farmers, the farm workers and the Foxes all move slowly as the small fox, lost and terrified, is spotted by Boggis and the farm workers

The farm workers close in, approaching the stage and shining their torches on the small fox, who freezes, rooted to the spot

When the small fox is surrounded, Boggis approaches till he is very close to the small fox. He slowly raises his shotgun. As he is about to pull the trigger…

Suddenly we hear a loud creaking sound. The tree us becomes visible. It is swaying ominously, uprooted by all the digging

Badger appears; as Narrator he doesn't have to observe the slow motion

Badger (*shouting*) Look out! The tree! The tree!

Perhaps strobe lighting heightens the tension as the tree, in slow motion, starts to fall. Bunce and Bean back away their tractors, and the farm workers, in slow motion, break ranks and scatter

The small fox is still rooted terrified to the spot. Boggis is still aiming the shotgun at him, but is several times nudged by fleeing farm workers, thus losing his aim

Suddenly Mr Fox appears, in slow motion, and approaches his son. In the nick of time he scoops him up in his arms and carries him off to safety. They exit

Boggis, too late, fires his shotgun, just as the tree, which has been tottering slowly but surely, falls on him, knocking him to the ground

The strobe and the slow motion stop. The animals, led by Badger, cheer as Boggis frees himself and beats a deflated retreat

Our story's now just half-way through.
So come back soon and see Part Two!

Happy music strikes up and Badger leads the animals off through the auditorium or off stage

N.B. In the original production the fall of the tree proved to be so dramatic and excitingly theatrical that Badger's final couplet and the jolly departure of the animals seemed quite inappropriate. A Black-out and a sudden silence left the audience in a momentary state of shock! And Boggis freed himself after the House Lights had come up. It seems to me that both endings work, depending on the style of the production

<h3 style="text-align:center">END OF ACT I</h3>

ACT II

Music strikes up. With the House Lights up, the company of animals return through the auditorium, encouraging the audience to clap in rhythm. Then they climb up on to the tabletop and dance. Some of the younger animals play games like leapfrog, or cheekily pull each others' tails

As the music comes to an end, all cheer and return to their seats as Badger takes the floor

N.B. In the original production the company were discovered on stage with no dancing entr'acte

Badger Welcome back, my fellow diggers and (*to the audience*) our friends, to Part Two of...

All FANTASTIC MR FOX!

Badger You will remember, I hope, that in their desperate quest to kill Mr Fox, the farmers with their tractors and mechanical shovels went to work, biting huge mouthfuls out of the hill. The big tree under which the Fox family lived was toppled like a matchstick. The hole the machines had dug was like the crater of a volcano. The hill had all but disappeared.

Adult Animals A crime! Disgraceful! A crime! Shameful!

Badger A crime indeed. But were the farmers satisfied? They were not. They switched off the engines of their tractors and walked to the small foxhole in the bottom of the huge crater.

The farmers enter from US, *carrying their guns and camping stools and picnic baskets*

Animals (*chanting*) Boggis and Bunce and Bean
　　　　　　　　　One fat, one short, one lean.
　　　　　　　　　These horrible crooks
　　　　　　　　　So different in looks
　　　　　　　　　Were still just as equally mean!

They boo. The farmers ignore them, then put down their gear

Boggis Dang and blast that filthy, stinking fox. What the heck do we do now?

Bean I'll tell you what we *don't* do. We don't let him go!

Boggis Never, never, never! (*With each "never" he extravagantly punches the air, hitting Bean and Bunce*)

Bean (*looking down the hole*) Did you hear that, Mr Fox? It's not over yet, Mr Fox. We're not going home till we've strung you up dead as a dingbat! (*To the others*) Agreed?

Boggis & Bunce Agreed!

Bunce So what's the next move?

Bean We're sending you down the hole to fetch him up!

Bunce What?

Bean and Boggis pick up Bunce and start swinging him towards the hole

Bean Down you go, you miserable midget!

Bunce No! No! Not me!

Bean and Boggis drop Bunce on the ground. He reacts angrily. The animals laugh

Bean (*conspiratorially beckoning*) Listen.

Boggis and Bunce approach Bean from opposite directions. Bean raises his head and Boggis and Bunce's heads bump into each other. They react

There's only one thing to do. We've tried shooting him.

Boggis & Bunce Bang, bang!

Bean We've tried digging him out.

Boggis & Bunce Dig, dig!

Bean So now we ... *starve* him out. We camp here day and night watching the hole. Agreed?

Boggis & Bunce Agreed!

They start erecting their camping stools

Boggis (*suddenly*) Hang on!

Bean & Bunce What?

Boggis What if the fox digs a hole right through the hill and comes out on the other side? You didn't think of that one, did you?

Bean (*playing for time*) Of course I did.

Bunce Go on, then, tell us the answer.

Bean (*having an idea*) We'll order all our farm workers to surround the hill, each with a flashlight and a weapon...

Boggis (*enthusiastically*) ...sticks and guns...

Bunce ...and hatchets and pistols...

Bean ...and crowbars and pitchforks!
All Yes! Yes!

They provocatively celebrate. The animals boo. Then the farmers sit and settle. Badger steps forward

Badger So the order went down to the farmers. The workers formed a tight ring around the bottom of the hill. Escape for the fox, or indeed for any other animal, was now quite impossible. For three days and nights the waiting game went on. The farmers took it in turns to sleep. They'd brought food to eat and cider to drink.

The farmers eat from their picnic baskets. Boggis dangles a piece of chicken near the hole

Boggis Can you smell this, Mr Fox? Lovely tender chicken! Come and get it!
Badger The rich scent wafted down the tunnel...

Music as the scene changes to the foxhole, where the fox family crouch

Fox Child 1 Dad, I can smell chicken!

All the children sniff hungrily

Fox Children Mmmm! Chicken!
Fox Child 2 Mum, couldn't we just sneak up and snatch it?
Mrs Fox Don't you dare. That's just what they want us to do.
Fox Child 1 But I'm so *hungry*.
Fox Child 2 And thirsty. I want a drink.
Fox Children Please!
Mrs Fox (*whispering to Mr Fox*) What are we going to do? We've not eaten for days.
Mr Fox I know, I know. I'm thinking. I'm thinking.
Fox Child 1 Couldn't we make a dash for it?
Fox Child 2 We'd have a little bit of a chance, wouldn't we?
Mrs Fox (*snapping*) No chance at all. We're not going up there to face those guns. I'd sooner we stay down here and die in peace.

A doom-laden silence. Suddenly Mr Fox stirs

Mr Fox I wonder...
The Others What?
Mr Fox I've just had a bit of an idea!

Pause

Mrs Fox Go on then!
Fox Children Tell us!
Mr Fox Well, if we … no, it's no good. It won't work.
Mrs Fox Why not?
Fox Children Why not, Dad?
Mr Fox Because it means more digging and we're not strong enough for
    more digging.
Fox Children We are, Dad! We are!
Mr Fox Then let's do it!

Music as the Foxes start to dig in a sideways direction

Animals Digga digga dig!
        Digga digga dig!
        Digga digga digga
        Dig.

Suddenly Mrs Fox collapses, exhausted. Mr Fox springs to her aid

Mrs Fox I'm sorry, I'm so sorry. I don't think I'm going to be much help.
Mr Fox You stay right here, my love. Get your strength back. We won't be
    long!

*Music. The Lighting focuses on the Foxes digging and Badger on the
tabletop, allowing Mrs Fox and the farmers above to exit*

*During the following, on the tabletop the scene is set for Boggis's chicken
house*

Badger Mr Fox and his children started to dig once again.

The animals chant under Badger's narration

Animals Digga digga dig!   **Badger** This time Mr Fox chose a
        Digga digga dig!   special direction for the digging.
        Digga digga digga digga   Sideways and downwards.
        Dig dig dig!   Sideways and downwards. The
            work went more slowly now. But
        Digga digga dig!   they kept at it with great courage,
        Digga digga dig!   and little by little the tunnel began
        Digga digga digga digga   to grow.
        Dig dig dig!

(*Rising to a climax*)   *The digging continues*
Digga digga dig!
Digga digga dig!   Further, further, further they dug.
Digga digga digga digga   Now upwards, upwards, upwards
Dig dig dig!   towards the surface. Till at last...

Mr Fox Hold it!

The digging stops

I think, my dears, we're here!
Fox Children Where?
Mr Fox A place so marvellous you will go crazy with excitement! Let's see, let's see... (*He reaches up to the tabletop, slowly pushes open a trapdoor, and pokes his head up and through it*)

On the tabletop the scene has been set for Boggis's chicken house. Perhaps some of the animals hold painted cloths with holes through which the animal children can peep (as chickens) or perhaps a flat flies in with cages, the doors of which open to reveal puppet chickens, operated by some of the animals. Or perhaps the animals stand with their backs to the audience to suggest the wall of the chicken shed. Perhaps the animals make chicken noises. Perhaps they hold chicken puppets. Or (perhaps the simplest solution) the animals stay seated round the tabletop, operating chicken puppets on the edge

As yet, however, the chickens are not visible

I've done it! I've done it first time! (*He helps the fox children up through the trap door*) Look, children! Come up and see where you are! What a sight for hungry foxes! Boggis's Chicken House Number One!

Suddenly the chickens appear, clucking loudly

Exactly where I was aiming for! Yes!
Fox Children (*leaping with excitement*) Yes! Yes! Yes!

They scatter, heading for the chickens, who react loudly

Mr Fox Wait! Behave! Calm down! Let's do this properly.

The Fox children return

First, we drink!

He leads the children to a water trough upstage. They all kneel down and make enjoyable slurping noises. Then they all turn round

Stay there!

First he goes round the row of chickens, who shrink back in alarm. Then he goes behind the backing flat or cloth. We hear the sudden squawk of a deftly killed chicken. Then another. Then a third

Mr Fox emerges carrying three limp chickens. The children excitedly run to him, jumping up

No fooling. Back to the tunnel, quick!

Music as the foxes descend through the trap door

The Lights fade down on the tabletop and fade up on the tunnel

Mr Fox hands the three chickens to the oldest child

Take these back to your mother. Tell her to prepare a feast! Tell her the rest of us will be along in a jiffy, as soon as we've made a few other little … arrangements. Go!

The fox child starts to exit along the tunnel

Come on, my dears! Onward! Onward!

The foxes dig again

Animals Dig! Dig! Dig!

The Lighting fades on them and picks up the Small Fox hastening back down the tunnel

Badger The Small Fox ran back along the tunnel as far as he could, carrying the three plump chickens. He had a long way to run, but never stopped once.

The small fox reaches his mother, who is asleep

Small Fox Mummy! Mummy! Wake up! Wake up! Look!

Mrs Fox wearily looks up

Mrs Fox I'm dreaming! (*She goes back to sleep*)
Small Fox You're not dreaming, Mummy! Look!

Mrs Fox wakes up

They're real chickens! We're saved! We're not going to starve!
Mrs Fox But how on earth? Where did you get them?
Small Fox Boggis's Chicken House Number One! We tunnelled right up under the floor and Dad said to bring them home to you and prepare a feast!
Mrs Fox (*recovering her strength*) A feast it shall be, then! Oh, what a fantastic fox your father is! Well, don't just stand there! Let's get plucking!

The Lighting fades

Optional: music as the three farmers are seen patiently, determinedly waiting for Mr Fox to be starved out. This would not be a scene as such, just a fleeting reminder of the farmers and their situation

The animals start chanting. Lights up on Mr Fox and the three fox children, digging onwards

Animals   Digga digga dig!
                    Digga digga dig!
                    Digga digga digga digga
                    Dig dig dig!

                    Digga digga dig!
                    Digga digga dig!
                    Digga digga digga digga...

Suddenly a booming voice stops them in their tracks

Voice of Badger Who goes there?

The foxes freeze. Tension music

Badger (as a character now) becomes visible in the tunnel. His small son accompanies him

Mr Fox Badger, it's you!
Badger Foxy! My goodness me, I'm glad I've found someone at last. We've been digging around and around in circles for three days and nights and I haven't the foggiest idea where we are! This is my son, by the way. (*He pushes him forward*)

Mr Fox (*introducing them*) My brave children.
Fox Children Hallo.

The badger boy hides shyly behind his father's legs

Badger He's a bit shy, I'm afraid. And in a right old state, like me. Like
     everyone.
Mr Fox What do you mean, old friend?
Badger Haven't you *heard* what's happening up on the hill? Or what little's
     left of it. It's chaos. Half the wood has disappeared and there are men with
     guns everywhere. None of us can get out, even at night! We're all starving
     to death.
Mr Fox Who is *we*?

*The Lighting fades up on the tabletop. As each animal is mentioned, he or she
stands and mounts the tabletop, making a tableau*

Badger All us diggers. Mole. Rabbit. Their wives and children. Even Weasel
     and his family. Weasel can usually sneak out of the tightest spots, but not
     this time. They're desperate, Foxy, desperate.

*Music as we focus on the tabletop, where the animals perform a stylised
mime. Bewildered, tired and starving, they wander around like disorientated
refugees, searching for food and shelter. As soon as they think they have
found an escape route in any direction, they are stopped in their tracks by the
sight of the farm workers who appear all around the tabletop like sinister
shadows. Perhaps they shine torches on the dimly-lit animals. Eventually the
farm workers disappear as the animals form a final frozen tableau of despair.
They remain visible as the Lighting returns to the tunnel*

   What on earth are we going to do, Foxy? I think we're finished.
Mr Fox My dear old Badger, this mess everyone's in is all my fault.
Badger (*crossly*) I *know* it's your fault. And the farmers won't give up till
     they've got you. Unfortunately this means *us* as well. It means everyone
     on the hill.

*The tableau above unfreezes and the animals shuffle back to their seats
around the tabletop*

*During the following, on the tabletop the scene is set for Bunce's storehouse.
Again, this is created by the animals or with a flown backcloth. Rows of
plucked geese and ducks*

   (*Softly*) We're done for.

Badger's wife and family are the last to move

My poor wife is so weak she can't dig another yard.

Mr Fox Nor can mine. And yet, Badger, at this very minute she is preparing for me and my children the most delicious feast of plump, juicy...

Fox Children Chickens!

Badger Stop! Don't tease me! I can't stand it.

Mr Fox We're not teasing!

Fox Children It's true!

The small badger looks happier

Mr Fox And because everything is entirely my fault, I invite you to share the feast, I invite *everyone* to share it—you and Mole and Rabbit and Weasel and all your wives and children! There'll be plenty to go round, I promise!

Badger You mean it? You really mean it?

Mr Fox (*triumphantly*) Do you know where we've just been?

Badger Where?

Mr Fox Right inside Boggis's Chicken House Number One!

Badger No!

All The Foxes Yes!

Mr Fox But that's nothing to where we're going now. And you can come too, my dear Badger. You can help us dig.

Badger I will!

Mr Fox (*to Badger's son*) And your brave son can run back to Mrs Badger and all the others and spread the good news. Tell them they are invited to a Fox's Feast. Tonight! Off you go!

Small badger looks at his father, who nods

Small Badger Yes, Mr Fox.

Badger Say thank you.

Small Badger Thank you, Mr Fox.

Small badger scurries off down the tunnel and exits

Mr Fox Now, everyone! Dig!

Music as the foxes and Badger dig in a new direction. The animals chant

Animals   Digga digga dig!
                 Digga digga dig!

Digga digga digga digga
Dig dig dig!

Digga digga dig!
Digga digga dig!
Digga digga digga digga
Dig dig dig!

Mr Fox Hold it! (*He reaches up and finds another trapdoor*)
Badger How in the world can you know where we are?
Mr Fox I know my way around these farms blindfolded. It's just as easy
below ground as it is above it! (*He climbs up through the trapdoor*)

On the tabletop, the scene is set for Bunce's storehouse

Yes! I've done it again! On the nose!

*Badger follows. Two of the fox children sit by the trapdoor. The third stays
below*

Badger (*amazed*) Where are we?
Mr Fox Farmer Bunce's Mighty Storehouse! Ducks and geese mainly. Feast
your eyes on that!
Badger It's like a dream!

Badger and the young foxes spring forward to grab the food

Mr Fox Stop! We mustn't overdo it! Mustn't give the game away! Mustn't
let them know what we've been up to. We must be neat and tidy and take
three or four ducks and geese. No more.

*They start collecting some choice items, forming a conveyor belt to pass them
through the trap door to the second oldest fox child*

Badger (*suddenly*) Foxy, look! A side of bacon. I'm mad about bacon!
Might we er…
Mr Fox Why not, dear friend!
Badger Thank you! (*He collects the side of bacon and passes it down*)
Little Fox And carrots, Dad!
Mr Fox Don't be a twerp! We never eat things like that!
Little Fox Not for us. The Rabbits! They only eat vegetables.
Mr Fox My goodness, you're right! What a thoughtful little fellow you are!
Take ten bunches of carrots!

*The little fox does so and passes them down. The other children return down
the trapdoor, as Badger thoughtfully stops Mr Fox in his tracks*

Badger Foxy. (*Carefully*) Doesn't this worry you just a tiny bit?
Mr Fox Worry me? What?
Badger All this ... this stealing.
Mr Fox My dear old furry frump, do you know anyone in the whole wide
world who wouldn't swipe a few ducks or geese if his children were
starving to death?
Badger But ... stealing is wrong. Isn't it?
Mr Fox You are far too respectable.
Badger There's nothing wrong with being respectable.
Mr Fox Look. Boggis and Bunce and Bean are out to kill us!
Badger Indeed they are.
Mr Fox But we're not going to stoop to their level. We don't want to kill
them.
Badger I should hope not.
Mr Fox We wouldn't dream of it. We shall simply take a little food here and
there to keep us and our families alive. Right?
Badger I suppose so...
Mr Fox If they want to be horrible, let them. We down here are decent, peace-
loving creatures. Right?

Pause

Badger Right. Right.

They shake hands

Mr Fox Now, onward! Onward!

*They descend through the trapdoor. The animals chant as Badger narrates
and Mr Fox sends his second oldest child back to his mother. Then Mr Fox,
the two Fox children and Badger dig once more*

*During the following, the tabletop becomes Bean's cider cellar. Perhaps the
animals create it with cloths stretched between them depicting rows and rows
of cider jars. Or perhaps a flat or a cloth flies in*

Animals Digga digga dig!
Digga digga dig!   **Badger** Mr Fox told the Small Fox
Digga digga digga digga   to take the lovely loot back to his
Dig dig dig!   mother and to tell her that there

Digga digga dig!   would be guests for dinner and
Digga digga dig!   that it must truly be a great feast.
Digga digga digga digga   Meanwhile we set off down the
Dig dig dig!   tunnel for just one more visit...

Mr Fox Stop!

Music as Mr Fox pushes open another trapdoor above him. All climb up. The tabletop has become Bean's cider cellar. The intruders look about them

Badger (*whispers*) Where are we, Foxy?
Mr Fox This belongs to Farmer Bean.
Fox Child Can't see any turkeys.
Mr Fox We don't need any more food, my dear. This is Bean's Secret Cider Cellar!
Fox Children (*excitedly*) Cider!
Mr Fox Shhh! We're right under the farmhouse! Come on!

They tread carefully towards the cider jars

Suddenly from the shadows, emerges Rat. Or perhaps he could be up a ladder

Rat Hey! You lot!

The intruders jump back in surprise

Go away! You can't come in here! This is my private pitch! (*He drinks from a small cider jar with a rubber tube straw*)
Badger Good Lord! It's Rat.
Mr Fox He's drunk!
Rat Mind your own business! Go away! (*Petulantly*) I got here first!
Badger Calm down, Rat. There's enough for all of us!
Rat You're not getting any! If you great clumsy brutes come messing about in here we'll all be caught!
Mr Fox If you don't shut up, *I'll* catch you and gobble you up! (*He advances*)

Rat backs away, dropping his cider jar

Rat I'm warning you!
Mr Fox Try me.
Rat It's not fair! I'll get my friends on you!

Mr Fox advances again

Rat squeals and disappears

One of the fox children picks up the cider jar and takes a gulp

Mr Fox (*to Badger*) I didn't think Rat *had* any friends!
Badger He's no friend of mine.
Fox Child Wow! This is some cider!

The second fox child starts to take a swig

Mr Fox (*taking the jar*) That's quite enough of that! (*He drinks some*) You're right, though. It's beautiful! It's fabulous! Your turn, Badger.

Badger drinks

Badger Oh! It's like melted gold! Like drinking sunbeams and rainbows!
Mr Fox Now, two jars each! Quickly!

Music as the foxes and Badger approach the jars. They find some (behind the cloths?) and creep back towards the trapdoor

Suddenly we become aware of Rat and three of his rat friends or children following behind

The audience may shout a warning. In any event, suddenly the Rats spring and pounce on the Foxes and Badger. Perhaps two of them leap on the backs of Mr Fox and Badger. Perhaps the others wrestle with the Fox children. The animals round the tabletop shout encouragement as a fight breaks out. The jars are fought over. The Rats seem to be losing, chased off by Mr Fox and Badger, but suddenly we see that the small foxes are being overpowered by the rats

Fox Children Dad! Dad!
Rat (*shrieking*) I warned you! I warned you!
Mr Fox Let them go! (*He springs to his children's defence*)

Suddenly all are stopped in their tracks. A loud door slam echoes from above, followed by loud footsteps clomping down the stairs. After a frozen pause, all dash to hide. Tension music

The Rats exit

The small Foxes hide behind the cloth. Mr Fox and Badger hide DS in the shadows

The footsteps stop. Enter Mabel, farmer Bean's plump housekeeper

Mabel Yes, Farmer Bean, certainly, Farmer Bean, three bags full, Farmer Bean. I'd just love to go down them rickety stairs into that there cellar all dark and parky cold. Why can't he fetch his own silly cider? "Two jars, Mabel," he orders like some posh squire. "Two jars to last me the day!" Who does he think I am. (*Shouting up the stairs*) I'm your housekeeper, not your cellar skivvy! (*She trips and stumbles*) Oooof! Farmer Bean, you'll be the death of me. You'll finish me off good and proper even if you can't finish off that fox! (*She gets up*) "It's starving, Mabel", he says. "Bound to make a run for it today!" Huh! After two jars of cider, he won't hardly see it let alone see it off! Now then, where be them jars? (*She turns on a torch and, shining it, searching, she approaches near where Mr Fox is hiding*)

Tension music

But I'll be glad when the rotten brute be killed and strung up on the front porch. Maybe I could have his head. (*With a chuckle*) Could stuff it and hang it on my bedroom wall!

Mr Fox reacts. Badger restrains him. Mabel moves away and finds the jars

There they be!

She goes to pick up two, then stops and sniffs. Tension music increases

Ugh. Mabel, there be rats down here again. Yes, I can sniff 'em, filthy creatures. Uggggh! Rats, I hate 'em. Where's that poison, Mabel? Eh? Where, where, where…? (*She finds a large packet marked "rat poison"*) Ah! Got it! (*She puts some in a bowl and places it* c) Come on! Come on! Come and get it, you verminous little rodents. Tasty turkey-flavoured poison. Yummy, yummy, yummy. Good riddance. (*She starts to leave. Suddenly*) Oh! Dang it! Nearly forgot Farmer Bean's cider. (*She fetches it and starts to exit*) Dear oh dear, Mabel! You'll forget your own name soon. (*Laughing*) Come on, Mavis, upstairs!

Mabel exits, hooting with laughter at her own joke. Footsteps echo. Followed by a loud door slam

Tension music continues as the two Fox children emerge innocently and sniff the turkey-flavoured poison. Ravenous, they excitedly head for the bowl. Hopefully the audience shout a warning. In any event, Mr Fox sees

Mr Fox No! (*He dashes up and ushers them away*) It's poison!
Fox Child 3 Sorry, Dad.
Fox Child 4 It smelt of turkey!
Mr Fox High time we went home. Ready, Badger?

They grab some cider jars

Badger Ready!

*Music as they climb down through the trapdoor. They start walking on the
spot*

*Optional: At this point we might once again briefly see the farmers.
Frustratedly but doggedly waiting, waiting*

Badger resumes his narrator role

(*To the audience*) Along the tunnel we flew. Past the turning that led to
Bunce's Mighty Storehouse, past Boggis's Chicken House, and then up
the long home stretch towards the place where Mrs Fox and Mrs Badger
would be waiting.
Mr Fox We'll soon be there! What a feast we'll have!
Badger And just think what we're bringing home in these jars! Mrs Badger
will be delighted!
Mr Fox And Mrs Fox!

They all continue walking on the spot

> (*Singing*) Home again swiftly I glide
> Back to my beautiful bride.
> She'll not feel so rotten
> As soon as she's gotten
> Some cider inside her inside!

Mr Fox, Badger & Fox Children She'll not feel so rotten
> As soon as she's gotten
> Some cider inside her inside!

Badger   Oh poor Mrs Badger, she cried
> So hungry she very near died.
> But she'll not feel so hollow
> If only she'll swallow
> Some cider inside her inside!

All Four   But she'll not feel so hollow
                 If only she'll swallow
                 Some cider inside her inside!

                 Cider inside her
                 Cider inside her
                 Cider inside her inside!
                 Cider inside her
                 Inside her
                 Inside her
                 Cider inside her inside!

Music builds as the four travellers exit and the Lighting focuses on the tabletop, where all the animals gather for the feast

The food is brought on (perhaps painted or attached to a tablecloth). All sing

Animals   Cider inside her
                 Cider inside her
                 Cider inside her inside!
                 Cider inside her
                 Inside her
                 Inside her
                 Cider inside her inside!

                 Home again swiftly I glide
                 Back to my beautiful bride
                 She'll not feel so rotten
                 As soon as she's gotten
                 Some cider inside her inside!

                 Cider inside her
                 Cider inside her inside!
                 Cider inside her
                 Inside her
                 Inside her
                 Cider inside her inside!

Mr Fox, the two Fox children and Badger arrive from US

Mr Fox Welcome, diggers all, to Fox's feast!

All cheer and welcome home the travellers. The cider is passed out and poured into the drinking vessels as Mr Fox approaches Mrs Fox

> (*Singing*) Home again I have arrived
> Back to my beautiful bride.

He embraces her. The fox children join them

All   She'll not feel so rotten
                 As soon as she's gotten
                 Some cider inside her inside!

Badger approaches Mrs Badger

Badger   Oh poor Mrs Badger, she cried
                 So hungry she very near died.

They embrace. The badger children join them

All   But she'll not feel so hollow
                 If only she'll swallow
                 Some cider inside her inside!

                 Cider inside her
                 Cider inside her
                 Cider inside her inside!
                 Cider inside her
                 Inside her
                 Inside her
                 Cider inside her inside!

Badger A toast! Let us all drink a toast to our dear friend who has saved our
lives this day! Mr Fox!
All Mr Fox! Long may he live!

All drink, then cheer. As everybody returns to their seats...

Badger (*to the audience*) Then every digger feasted famously, till it was time
for Mr Fox to...
All Speech! Speech! Speech!

Mr Fox stands

Mr Fox My friends. Our delicious meal was courtesy of Farmers Boggis,
Bunce and Bean!

Hoorays and boos

They don't know it, but now we have a safe tunnel leading to the three finest food stores in the world! Theirs!

Cheers

We nearly starved because it was unsafe to go outside.
Badger Yes—we'd have been shot before we'd gone a yard!
Mr Fox Exactly. Our enemies are outside, but now we never need go outside again!

Cheers

We will make an underground village, with streets and homes on each side for Badgers and Moles and Rabbits and Weasels and Foxes. And every day I will go shopping for you. And every day we will eat like kings!

Cheers and applause. Mr Fox sits down. Badger stands

Badger (*to the audience*) And we do!
Mrs Fox (*leaping up*) Because my husband, my dear husband is…
All FANTASTIC MR FOX!

Cheers

The Lighting fades down. Thunder claps. Lightning flashes. A rain effect

On to the tabletop enter Boggis, Bunce and Bean with their guns

As Badger narrates, they sit C

Badger Outside the foxhole, Boggis and Bunce and Bean waited in the rain.
Boggis He won't stay down there much longer now.
Bunce The brute must be famished.
Bean He'll be making a dash for it any moment.
Badger They waited. And waited. And so far as I know, they are waiting still.

The Lights fade to Black-out

END OF ACT II

When the Lights come up, the animals dance in celebration, forcing the farmers to join in. Then they wave to the audience as they dance out of the auditorium

FURNITURE AND PROPERTY LIST

Further dressing may be added at the director's discretion

ACT I

On stage: Tabletop. *On it*: tablecloth, remains of a feast, drinking vessels
            Tree
            Mr Fox's sack

Off stage: Chicken (**Boggis**)
            Duck, goose (**Bunce**)
            Turkey, flagon of cider (**Bean**)
            Shotguns (**Boggis, Bunce** and **Bean**)
            Shovels (**Boggis, Bunce** and **Bean**)
            Torches (**Farm Workers**)
            Boggis's shotgun (**Farm Workers Leader**)
            Tractors equipped with mechanical shovels (**Bunce** and **Bean**)

Personal: **Mr Fox: detachable tail**

ACT II

On stage: As before

Off stage: Guns, camping stools, picnic baskets (**Boggis, Bunce** and **Bean**)
            Piece of chicken (**Boggis**)
            Painted cloths or flats with cages, chicken puppets (**Stage
               Management**)
            Rows of plucked geese, ducks, bacon and ten bunches of carrots in
            Bunce's storehouse (**Stage Management**)
            Bean's cider cellar depicting rows of cider jars, rubber tube straw,
              large packet marked "rat poison", bowl (**Stage Management**)
            Torch (**Mabel**)
            Food painted or attached to tablecloth (**Stage Management**)

LIGHTING PLOT

Practical fittings required: torches
Composite setting. The same throughout

ACT I

To open: General lighting, house lights up

Cue 1   **Animals** dance on tabletop   (Page 1)
                   Fade house lights

Cue 2   Music   (Page 3)
                   Bring up lighting on foxhole under tree

Cue 3   **Farmers** enter   (Page 3)
                   Bring up slightly subdued lighting on **Farmers**

Cue 4   **Fox Family** descend into their foxhole   (Page 5)
                   Fade lighting on **Fox Family**

Cue 5   **Farmers** unfreeze   (Page 5)
                   Brighten light on **Farmers**

Cue 6   **Farmers** exit   (Page 6)
                   Fade lighting on **Farmers***, bring up lighting on foxhole*

Cue 7   **Fox** exits   (Page 7)
                   Fade lights, then bring up general moonlight and light
                       on foxhole

Cue 8   **Farmers** exit   (Page 8)
                   Cross-fade to inside foxhole

Cue 9   **Mr** and **Mrs Fox** look encouragingly at each other   (Page 9)
                   Fade lights, then bring up light on tabletop

Cue 10   **Farmers** enter   (Page 9)
              Cross-fade to general moonlight

Cue 11   **Farmers** mime digging   (Page 9)
              Lights up in foxhole

Cue 12   **Mrs Fox** hugs **Mr Fox**   (Page 11)
              Fade lighting on foxhole and change to early morning sun
                  on tabletop

Cue 13   **Badger**: "…felt safe enough to rest."   (Page 13)
              Lighting on foxhole

Cue 14   **Farm Workers** enter   (Page 14)
              Dim lighting under tree area

Cue 15   Loud creaking sound is heard   (Page 16)
              Light on tree

Cue 16   **Badger**: "The tree! The tree!"   (Page 16)
              Optional strobe lighting

Cue 17   Tree falls   (Page 16)
              Cut optional strobe, change lighting

ACT II

To open: House lights up

Cue 18   **Animals** climb on to tabletop   (Page 18)
              Cross-fade to tabletop

Cue 19   **Badger**: "The rich scent wafted down the tunnel…"   (Page 20)
              Lights on foxhole

Cue 20   **Mr Fox**: "We won't be long!"   (Page 21)
              Lighting on **Foxes** *digging and* **Badger** *on tabletop*

Cue 21   **Foxes** climb up through trap door   (Page 22)
              Fade lights on tunnel

Cue 22   **Foxes** descend through the trap door   (Page 23)
              Cross-fade to tunnel

Cue 23   **Animals**: "Dig! Dig! Dig!"   (Page 23)
          Fade lighting on **Animals**; *spot on* **Fox Child** *hastening*
              back down tunnel

Cue 24   **Mrs Fox**: "Let's get plucking!"   (Page 24)
          Fade lighting

Cue 25   **Farmers** wait   (Page 24)
          Optionally briefly bring up lights on **Farmers**

Cue 26   **Animals** start chanting   (Page 24)
          Lights up on **Mr Fox** *and* **Fox Children**

Cue 27   **Mr Fox**: "Who is *we*?"   (Page 25)
          Fade up lighting on tabletop

Cue 28   **Animals** form a final frozen tableau   (Page 25)
          Lighting focus on tunnel, but **Animals** *on tabletop visible*

Cue 29   **Farmers** wait   (Page 32)
          Optionally briefly bring up lights on **Farmers**

Cue 30   **Mr Fox**, **Badger** and **Fox Children** exit   (Page 33)
          Lighting focus on tabletop

Cue 31   **All** cheer   (Page 35)
          Fade lighting down, then lightning flashes with rain effect

Cue 32   **Badger**: "...they are waiting still."   (Page 35)
          Fade lights to black-out, then bring up lighting for finale

EFFECTS PLOT

ACT I

Cue 1	To open *Homespun folk music*	(Page 1)
Cue 2	The adult **Animals** drink a toast *Music introducing story*	(Page 2)
Cue 3	**Badger**: "…down into the valley…" *Music*	(Page 3)
Cue 4	**Farmers** freeze *Music*	(Page 5)
Cue 5	**Bean**: "My dear Bunce, I've already found it." *Sinister music*	(Page 6)
Cue 6	**Farmers** enter stealthily *Sinister music*	(Page 7)
Cue 7	**Bunce**: "Stand by!" *Tension music*	(Page 7)
Cue 8	**Mr Fox** makes for trapdoor *Shotguns fire*	(Page 8)
Cue 9	**Fox Children**: "Night, Mum." *Music*	(Page 9)
Cue 10	**Farmers** "We'll dig you out, we will we swear!" *Music*	(Page 9)
Cue 11	**Farmers** start to mime digging *Music, sounds of shovels striking tabletop threateningly*	(Page 9)
Cue 12	**Mr Fox** moves nearer noise *Sound of shovel breaking through*	(Page 10)

Cue 13   **Foxes** mime digging   (Page 10)
             Musical pulse, partly still menacing noise of shovels

Cue 14   **Farmers** slow down   (Page 11)
             Fade out sound of shovels

Cue 15   **Badger**: "...and looked at the vast hole."   (Page 12)
             Music

Cue 16   **Badger**: "...felt safe enough to rest."   (Page 13)
             Music

Cue 17   **Farm Workers** are ready in position   (Page 14)
             Tension music

Cue 18   **Boggis**: "Death to the fox!"   (Page 15)
             Sudden terrible roar of engines

Cue 19   **Bunce** and **Bean** start digging   (Page 15)
             Mechanical clanks and clangs, continuing

Cue 20   **Fox Child** remains as others head for exit   (Page 15)
             Noise ceases except for musical pulse for tension

Cue 21   **Boggis** is about to shoot   (Page 16)
             Loud creaking sound

Cue 22   **Badger**: "So come back soon and see Part Two!"   (Page 16)
             Happy music

ACT II

Cue 23   To open   (Page 18)
             Music

Cue 24   **Animals** dance   (Page 18)
             Fade out music when ready

Cue 25   **Badger**: "The rich scent wafted down the tunnel..."   (Page 20)
             Music

Cue 26   **Mr Fox**: "Then let's do it!"   (Page 21)
             Music

Cue 27   **Mr Fox**: "We won't be long!"   (Page 21)
            Music

Cue 28   **Mr Fox** "Back to the tunnel, quick!"   (Page 23)
            Music

Cue 29   Lighting fades   (Page 24)
            Optional music

Cue 30   **Foxes** freeze   (Page 24)
            Tension music

Cue 31   **Badger**: "They're desperate, Foxy, desperate."   (Page 25)
            Music

Cue 32   **Mr Fox**: "Now, everyone! Dig!"   (Page 26)
            Music

Cue 33   **Mr Fox**: "Stop!"   (Page 29)
            Music

Cue 34   **Mr Fox**: "Quickly!"   (Page 30)
            Music

Cue 35   **All** are stopped in their tracks   (Page 30)
            *Loud door slam echoing from above, followed by
                loud footsteps clomping down stairs*

Cue 36   **All** dash to hide   (Page 30)
            Tension music

Cue 37   **Mabel** approaches near where **Mr Fox** is hiding   (Page 31)
            Tension music

Cue 38   **Mabel** stops and sniffs   (Page 31)
            Increase tension music

Cue 39   **Mabel** exits   (Page 31)
            *Echoing footsteps, followed by loud door slam, tension
                music continuing*

Cue 40   **Badger**: "Ready!"   (Page 32)
            Music

Cue 41   **Mr Fox, Badger & Fox Children**: "...her inside!"   (Page 33)
            Music builds

Cue 42   **All** cheer   (Page 35)
            Thunder claps, lightning, rain effect